Hazardous Patterns and Strange Lines: Assorted Poems

Julian Harris

BookLeaf Publishing

India | USA | UK

Presentation by *BookLeaf Publishing*

Web: www.bookleafpub.com

E-mail: info@bookleafpub.com

ISBN: 9789363300989

First edition 2024

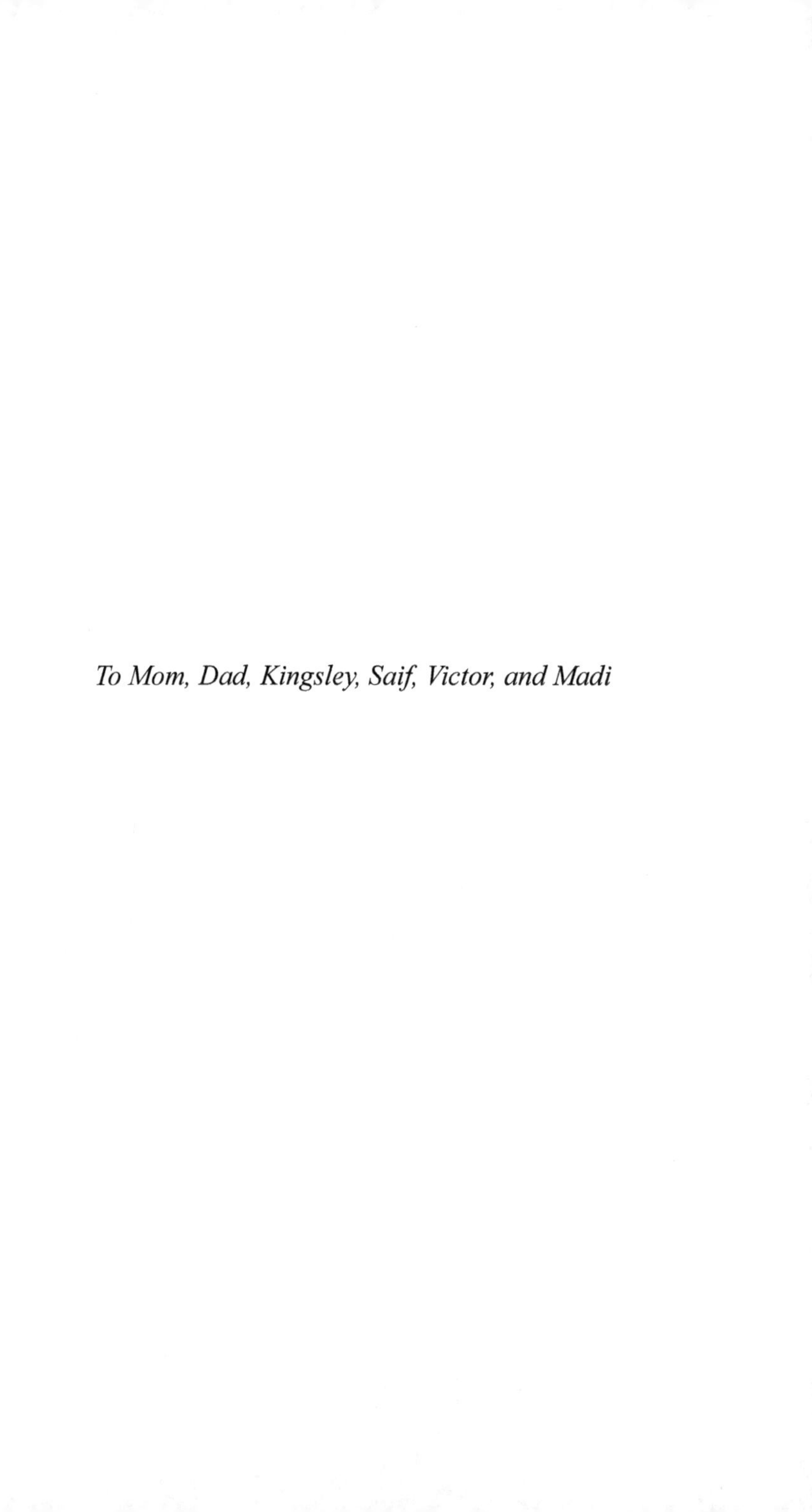

To Mom, Dad, Kingsley, Saif, Victor, and Madi

ACKNOWLEDGEMENT

Fuper Say
Finn
Adam Haan
Cole Gordon
Peter Mendiola
Dawn Smith
Ben Smith
Sidney
Dustin Christy
Bernard Cummings
KLV
Tiana Kaye Blair
Stan Wojewodski Jr
Blake Hackler
Sarah Romersburger
Shadow Wizards
Ron and Terry
Gramma
Matotts
Harris Family
Tragesers
Gia and Rick
SMU 2025 Ensemble and the Years surrounding

PREFACE

I hope you find something you like. I hope you make something better. I hope it crawls inside your head and lives with you.

Angels Envy the Makers Mark

I feel pity for the people
Who will spend their plentiful free time
Drinking and going out
Drinking for parties
Drinking with associates
Drinking in lovely suits and dresses
Drinking and going to fancy restaurants
Drinking and talking to people they barely know
Drinking and smoking cigarettes
Coming home and the first thing to greet them is
a drink
Finding it impossible to socialize without getting
a drink
Becoming so hollow from your occupation that
all you want is a drink
Drinking so much that you even lose the
pleasure of a drink
I feel pity for these people
Because I wish I was them

To the Tune of 80% Insurance Coverage

When they were
Digging in my mouth   (bristle drills
and shaking hands   Kept
worrying
The mirror drew back
I can hear his stomach churning)in the car
With tiny bits of me   "I need
a 21"   I could
just
I felt my gums give way to
"No, that's a 25"   Veer off
A pool, couldn't swallow it couldn't swallow it
He said it was "mad as hell" I thought funny
way to die   it was gonna hurt a lot and I said
wait it's gonna hurt a lot?
          My head was tilted, so it pooled
And the aid couldn't find the cotton
          I reached back with my tongue
                    She was nervous, kept dropping
things
She hadn't worked here often,
          Like salt, like sour, just tiny pinpricks
tiny   The company moves her around

Pinpricks   Placing little
wires, little wires Plucked from a pin cushion
"The water's not working"   We
talked about stick-and-poke, meaning for pain
        "The water's not working, we'll have to
move."   So I stumbled with my shades and
apron, a rubber lilly   I have
some modifications to make for sacrifices made
Clamped onto my lips
An elastic porthole to the pulp
And my body has a new message

Ultimatum

I hold my breath when you speak
Does it make me ready, prepared?
Why would I resist and hold against
This love
What harm could words do me?
What harm could those words do me
Shrug it off, take a drink
Banter with friends, backtalk
The squabbles watered by binding vows
Secrecy to exhalation till the hot
Lingering air funnels raggedly out of me
Scorching my throat and straining my voice
Smoke bringing tears and haggard sobs
As I seek out air untainted by cowardice
But that smell lingers in the house
A bad habit haunts the car
But for you, but for you
I hold my breath

Forward

With great blue fire and yawning wounds
The long dead seek solace in the hearts of the
new millennium
Those never satisfied, beautiful in form
Sculpted to the finest point, smooth yet firm
Nestled in their warm thundering chambers
Cuckoo zygote, pounds loud on the caged drum
Go forth! Go forth! Seek what I could not!
A name! A name! The only thing that lives
beyond you
What's yours and never was
Free to flit, infect the ears with blue flame
So their hearts may sing again

For those dead and yet dying

To all those who stare at the mirror
Or flex their hands to feel them
Who think the world is nothing but mouths
It is the divine comedy
That in a world of consumption
You will burn your fingers
While taking pizza out of an oven

Rent Day

Something knocks on a hingeless door
And in the uninterrupted humming of countless
electric observers you step to a concrete balcony
to rest on a frigid railing
Beholden to a midnight sun
A purple night burnt orange
No sleep
Much to do
An organ is an instrument and a tool
The vibration remains from blows received
Begone
To lightless rooms
This moment always escapes
Filled with wanting
No air nor drink nor mineral can kill
The memory
Release the railing
Return
Much to do
Always left craving
something
beyond the noise
The hum
Subdued jinns we are fool enough to trick
Taste of tongues and tuning forks

The final freedom of severance
Find comfort in a lightless room
Or we are all damned to a singular
No
It only feels like dying if you overthink it
At the least
You witnessed something so perfect and pure
Never could have sensed it.
Return
And again
And again
And again
You find your way back to a skyline
In a house with no exit
You hear a song replaced by its shadow
Fleeting, no exchanging it
No compensation
And costs for time lost
There was a melody.
To sleep
To sleep and return again.
Again.
Again.
Until

Nonexistent Needs in Requisite Times

And why not?
To live a life full of regret and mishap
And why not?
To be thankful for every day for the grace of
experience and being alive?
And why not?
To blame circumstance for mishap
For the tutelage of parents and the world that
encloses you
Why not
Cry out against
Your inability to choose
Your own regrets and mistakes
Why couldn't you do better
To realize something you must sacrifice for
After the sacrifice of many others
Only to be struck dead by something
Completely unexpected
What then
Do you ask faith?
Logic?
A predetermined reason?
What then?
What make of it then?

A single solution?
A broad question?
What then? What then?
What truth survives the changing times and the
drifting wants of an unsatisfied soul?
What do you give to one who thirsts but drinks
plenty water?
Can you? Will you? Should you? Would you?
Or give faith to the impulses of an internal
compass to drift amongst the tumultuous sea
Hoping if not for a simple island to rot in idle
bliss
A ravenous wave to make peace with

The Singing Bomb

A metal chasis
Filled with killing points
In the center a fairy
Celestial cephalopod crustacean
Wings of sea glass
Bioluminescent flutterings
Segmented limbs set in prayer
Marvel it's mimic face
False eyes and red lips
Porcelain doll
Chirriping mouth, pulling appendage
Compound eyes disguised
Chemical gown, gossamer gold
Each leg, pegged, a great chitin clockwork
Stirs and plucks wiry hairs
A tune
A hymn
If its prison filled its purpose on arrival
Fatal lines invade
A final note is struck
And all life returns to nature
No more cognizant than flowers or stones
A perfect way to steal a place
When all the houses and grain lay unharmed
But now it rests

Lodged in a forgotten place
But never
Safe

Longlegs Review

There is nothing to do but wait in a world of
sand
And there are plenty of rocks on a beach to build
small forts to live in
When I am hungry I hope I will have enough
money to eat
When I am in the car I cannot think about dying
When I am with my friends their eyes glisten in
the street light
I eat other animals and I eat plants
If my friends turn against me could I eat them
too?
Would you?
Could you?
Should you?
Is killing a sin? If you had to, would all the
shame in your heart build a damn to save the
poor and downtrodden? Could you lift both the
stones and the water and snot that you swallow
from your tears?
Do you need to whip the horse to make it move
faster?
Is a child without instruction doomed to
insolence?
Spare the rod spoil the whole bunch

Rotting rotting rotting
Baby bubble drowning daughter
Isaac and his father
Medea and her young
Blind your eyes and kiss your mother
The consequences follow even when you're
gone

Grand Reprise

The weight of tethered ghosts pull my esophagus
Down, down, like a tree sucked into the crushing
earth
Returned to simple fear
In the carnivorous world
Is there an escape
If every side will be challenged
And no state is permanent?
Trust in this thing beyond dust

Enter the Worm

I want you I want you I want you to
Stop pulling away and pushing it out with the
Rib that I gave and is forcefully shoved when
It's harder to think when you're carving it
through and the
Patience I've built has been making me lose it
for
Over the years I can't tell if we're making ends
meet
Or are we just scared of nothing after the ending.

Sin Eaters

"We get dirty so the world stays clean."
The devil you know
The lesser evil
The shame that colors blood like roses
If it is vile
If it is dangerous
They are fool enough to miss the devils that hide
And use sweet honey to open mouths
Stick in fingers caress wet holes
Aren't we guilty?
Self control, lack of will, a failure of restraint
Or a lack of understanding?
A physical draw, overwhelming, death for
denial?
Still separate from an animal?
The greatest saints for shuttering vice
Partake in quiet closets
Fresh shipment, off the dock
Showing the scapegoat is a scapegoat
A cue ball knocking cue balls in a dark room
Let no ideology maintain that there is no choice
Then it truly will be dead, and in appealing to
the court of forests we abide its rules

Song of Doom

Once more, once more
I will raise my family blade and cut my ties from
this world
Those who do not support me will feel the heel
of my boot upon their neck
I will kill not only their body but their name
I will change it to that of shame
Their gods, their people, made an example of
And any who would lend them aid will mark
their fingers with their foulness
I will see them severed
I will see their homes shattered and burned
Their children, put to the rack
Anything they make will be a representation of
the devil
Their dreams, the plot to doom all common
people
I will go beyond eradication, I will damn them
I will break their bones and contort them into
myth and monsters
Their stitched lips only howl like dogs
This I do for you
My love
Then all will be well
And then
And then

Bla Bla Post Modern
Preacher Post Modern Choir

Is it enough
Did you leave you mark
Did you finally do what could not be done
before
So now what's next
Do you do it all again
Do you work yourself to the bone for a dream
that might
Cost you more than what it would give
How can you tell if you've made an impact
How can you tell that the words they tell you are
true?
Haven't you tasted those white lies as well
Haven't you put on that smiling mask
Haven't you wondered if the thoughts in your
head are reactionary or controlled
Do you do things because you think you out to
Or does you body decide it first
If you think about crashing the car hard enough
Does it prepare you for when it does
Are you sick and tired of being sick and tired
Are you
Fed up with constant indignation

There's a thousand hundred reasons why you
shouldn't
Do what
You've been
Doing
With your
Life
So is it good enough to just be humble
Is it good enough to be above the rest
Are you along for a short ride,
a game,
a bright candle
Or are you
Just
Making excuses why you put others in pain
Are you ever satisfied with being satisfied
Do you recognize your own recognition
If you think thoughts upon thoughts upon
thoughts
Can you
Build a doorway out of your head
Are you lonely with others around you
Are you lonely when there's no one in bed
Do you constantly struggle with the concept that
one day you'll all be dead
And that the worst thing that ever could happen
You realize that it's all been said
So line dance if you must or make it a tango

It doesn't matter what side you choose if
everyone's got an angle
If you can't lead a horse to water and force it to
drink
Better
Bash in its skull because you can't make it think
Do people choose to change ideas like a new
pair of shoes
Or is it something that inevitably grows out of
you?
It's impossible to reason with an unreasonable
mind
With
questions on questions and no answers to find
If a final word is what you seek
than you best get in line
There's plenty motherfuckers who will give you
their time

So trust in what you want to
And be comfy on what hill you die
Cause at the end of the day
There's only so many words to say
Until it's all cliche
and you'll never know if it matters anyway.

(Post Comment: Bullshit, there were people on
the moon.)

Nothing, Nowhere, Not at All

Momentary flash
Banging on the ceiling
And the bones of my heels thud against the floor
which is a ceiling of someone else
Living below beneath below below
Down down
A person as I am
Seeing through eyes or seeing through nothing
1 and 2s
1 and 2s
Reds and blues
Reds and blues
In a contrast of colors I stand at the edge
The brief flash sublimating all of the dark
And in the next, all succumb to black
And again
And again
Brief flash
Full dark
And again
And again
This consistent pattern
Back
Again
Back

Again
I draw on my skin
Words with no meaning
And there is no reason save for a buzzing
That keeps me from sleep
I drew a road on my wall
With a mound and a tree
Where two men may lie waiting
For someone who never will arrive
If I could push past that membrane
Between the light and the dark
Between the nothing and the not at all
And fall into
An endless somersault
Would freedom be pleasant?
Or more vertigo?

Maybe picking at the seam
Does not reveal a deeper self
But unravels what you have
Spinning world of shapes and colors
Endless light in all directions
How close are you
To losing it all
One last drop
One more slip
The ice pick special
And who is left?
Who continues?

The Long Dead

Souls are often depicted as airy and light
Something beyond us, out of touch
Wouldn't it be unfortunate if our soul was a hard
pearl
Forced to float down a river
Or be shut forever in a tomb
The great thing about air
Is that is will eventually leave the body
Well
For most

The Gut

Turning Turning
The shit I put down the shit I spew out
Turning Turning
I was always car sick
Now I'm plain sick
And I think and I think
Just keep it down keep it down
I need to prove I can do it
Prove mind over matter
But then the doubt creeps in
You'll feel better if you get it out
One and done
But I'm a dry heaver
Even when there's nothing left in me
There is the feeling
GET IT OUT GET IT OUT
Like reaching down a dog's throat
Spititoutspititout
The churning the churning the churning
Compression
The squeezing digestion
Half formed too green
Twist twist
Spin cycle hot water causes me to sweat
The steam the steam not that

Toilet bowl cleaner stench
Too clean too chemical makes
Me want
To
Retch
I was lying on the carpet
And the thoughts in my head didn't match with
the words in my mouth
Can't get up
"Aaah fuck"
Gotta get up
"Goddamnit"
You have to move
"Fuck it"
Who's in charge here who's in charge here come
on man MOVE YOU GOTTA GO
"Fuuuuuuuuuck"
Gut to spine fever sweat in the throat
Those burning bubbles like a hot rock sat out in
a Dallas Sun 104 104 runs through you like a
train run train on your head get fucked ha ha ha
ha
Digesting bark digesting corn husks broccoli
stems and apple cores
Makes me feel guilty to cough
Come on big man come on big guy
Get it together get it together

It takes guts and grit, gravel between your teeth
and you'll chew that asphalt until it comes out
your

The Gambler

I know it
I know it
The cards that I'm holding
Hearts are for lovers but this hand has debt
I'll shoot for the moon then soon end up
regretting
But chips on my shoulders are begging for use
What happened to "maybe" and anticipating
The monkeys know levers that work half the
time
But I can't lie waiting and lie that I'm waiting
For someone to save me before saving myself
What is this bullshit of self-serving sadness
The more you believe it the more you will see
And I'm getting tired of constant revolving
So on the next revolt, I'll see my way out
What are you saying? You go with what's given
And everyone's got their own interests at heart
Well your teeth are pointed and I'm sure you
could use them
But I feel great pity for the missing and marked
No one's a saint so you'd best be a soldier
You do your best work with the clothes they
adorn

Well sure I love orders when they're easily
followed
But I just can't handle the suit that I show
I could be a someone and shuffle my body
I'll set up the group and then teach them the
rules
But if I get too tired of grand old delusions
I'll be more insightful when you ask me again
I gotta
I gotta
Please hold onto something
There's something I need that continues beyond
But if it's all over
I know where I'm going
I'll come back around and then
See myself out
So show me a game that has no sore losers
Show me a game I can finally beat
And though it's all gimmicks and agreed upon
lies
I won't feel so guilty for starting again

How to Live Your Life with No Contradictions, Regrets, or Mistakes

They'll find a hundred cracks in your teeth
Curse them when you chip your molars
Biting down onto their collar bones
You should listen to your intuition
And kill those fuckers where they stand
Cause if it's eye for an eye
best go for right between em
Sure, there was no better option for us all

You should roll over
and let the jackals have at you
Let the opportunists prop their shacks up with
your skin
Let the squatters take over
In the pit of your stomach
From all the words that you swallowed instead
of said

Well it ain't all bad
It ain't all bad
The stuff you always worry about just keeps
making me so sad

If it's out of your control
Do the best with what you can
Don't try to be an asshole
If you can't confront what makes you scared
But if you have to put your foot down
Just make it quick

Coward's Love Song for a Bear

The bear dresses well
And has 5 different colognes
Cultivated in the arts
And a master of debate
Political know-how
And a sharp wit
Physical exercise
Inspired from model men
Bukowski and Hemingway on the shelf
Bravado and a penchant for Tom Jones
Wishes he was born in a past era
or that he could return to Europe
But fashions himself an American Animal
With Springsteen and a growing interest in
football
The bear drinks
The bear prides himself on drinking
Drinking as an art
Good old Oliver Reed
Flashing his special tattoo
Now that, that's an actor
That's a man
What happened to all the men
So sad, so sad

At the top of the tower
An unmatched intellect
Is it cold inside your walls of stone
And your echoing soul?
What stuffs the bear
When the liquor soaks the cotton
Monday Night Raw Arm Wrestling champion
A real killer
Could have been a soldier
Talks about his lack of empathy
And his need to conquer
But favors the soft animals
The women in his life who've treated him well
Oh if he could return to the good old days
The old boy times, when things were simple
Of small monitor screens and 4 am parties
Cheap Kroger wine and singing until your throat
caved in
Thunder Ball, Thunder Road
Always picking at himself
For a creature of confidence, the kings head
holds more than a crown
A killing dagger, hovering hangover
But hell of a hard worker
Certain to carve and to carve
The bear is strong
The bear makes a way through
In a conversation, in a set, in a scene
Pushing, pushing

The bear can spin a thread from the stitching in
his sides
A bullshit bit is better backed with a head that
holds some substance
Drunk on the street
Pick up the bear
Too sloppy to see the volume dial in the dark of
the dashboard
The bear sings with everything in him
The bear's a winner
The bear wants kids
A son
A real Conan
A Man's man
I don't speak like the bear
Words and actions jitter out of me
I need time
But the bear can take time
The bear breaks down time's door and kisses its
mother on the mouth
Not to say the bear doesn't have manners
Neat and tidy as a Christmas ribbon
Groomed to the teeth
And he's got plenty of them
A firm handshake and polite smiles
The bear's one weakness is the weakness of us
all
And it kills the bear with a certain melody

The same thing that keeps the bear together is
the same thing that binds him
Seams and stitches tight and taught him how to
do it right
He's sworn oaths and his sense of justice will be
known
Oh bear
Oh bear
Can't you see it?
You're indeed a mighty beast
What more do you have to prove?
I know you've read the greats
And would love to join them
Oh bear
What more can you do?
When your lovers turn to sand?
And your shoulder starts to mold
The sawdust leaking from your eyes
As you try to suck it in?
It's hard kicking those dogs down
When you're the king of the hill
Come on Titus, come on Caesar
You should read that book I gave you
The one of all the superpowers
And know the fate of all great men
Even the ones who smile
Cocksure and sure of it
Watch all the movies and know the lines
You'll be in the stars one day

Ursa Major deal
And a house at the beach
Watch the freaks on the walk
And at night become one
Piss on your shoes
And howl curses at the world
Because it is cold
It swirls around you
The Quantum Python
Time and Again
Swallow you whole
Back to the places you forgot
Or tried to
Take it easy, kid
You're not like the rest of us
You sure burn bright when your fur smells like
whiskey
And the smoke puffs rings between your rubbery
gums
Watch for those poor little souls you cause to
shriek
You may not think much if them, with your eyes
so high in your tower of you
But they could be someone else's soft one
Hell, who are they?
Why should you care?
You could kill em all, bear
Kill em all, big man
You know what's best for you

You grew up tough and your gemstone eyes
don't lie
There are harsh lines that cut the rules
But you're not the brother they make you
Not in this land at least
Burn it all and sing your songs
Drink your drink and swoon the girls
Georgie Porgy and drive it all to hell
When the LA precaution meets your 60th
birthday
I hope before that day
You can pick the gravel from your tear ducts
And tell me what's on your mind
And loosen up your threads
To let your cotton out
Cause hell, it was bound to happen one day
And for all the drink and movies
Have you released your greatest poison
Is the past?
I love you, bear.
Even when you push
Even when the smoke comes out your mouth
And when you can't find your way on the street
You don't need a girl
And you don't need me
You've got everything you need
Because you made it yourself
And all the flesh and all the gold
Will turn to stuffing sawdust and seaside sand

I hope you will remember the most perfect
wisdom of all
The subtle art found in all things
No word, nor tongue, nor wind could illuminate
The beauty of the silent world
And the faith of not knowing
Don't worry bear
You'll make it out
Even if you break your teeth from biting
Learn a lesson, stay a while
And shut your fackin' mouth.

It's Alright

..

..

..

..

....

....

....

....

....

....

.....

....

.....

....

....

....

....

....

....

....

...

...

...

......

....

,,·,·,
·,,,·,··,··,··,··,·,··
.,,··,··,?·,,·,···?··
.?·,··,,,?,··,??·,?.
,,!·??·,!··??·??·?,??·,?·,··
,?!·??!? ·,··,!!·!,!!!?,!!?,???????,
,,·??,?·!
!!!!!
!!
!
·
···
?
···????
?··
?!!
·
···
····,,
···,···
····,·,,,,,··
···
·
····
·
···
·
·

...
.
...
.